THE STORY OF JESUS

INTRODUCTION

© 2004 BY WILLIAM B. JONES, JR.
Author of Classics Illustrated: A Cultural History

The Story of Jesus, first published in December 1955 at a cover price of thirty-five cents, marked a milestone in the history of Classics Illustrated. It was the first of sixteen Special Issues that would appear under the yellow Classics banner in the late 1950s and early 1960s. Covering topics as different as the Prehistoric World, the American Civil War, and the Atomic Age, the Special Issues played a significant role in expanding the educational mission that Albert L. Kanter envisioned for the various comic-book series his Gilberton Company had launched since 1941.

The parent Classics Illustrated line (originally called Classic Comics) featured comics-style adaptations of literary masterpieces (*Don Quixote*, *Huckleberry Finn*, *Great Expectations*) and biographies of such figures as *Marco Polo*, *Benjamin Franklin*, and *Joan of Arc*. During an era when comic books were coming under increasing scrutiny by legislative committees and outright attack by cultural critics, Kanter made every effort to improve the quality of Classics Illustrated and to enhance its reputation as "the World's Finest Juvenile Publication."

In 1953, Kanter introduced two new comic-book series. Classics Illustrated Junior presented folk tales (*Johnny Appleseed*), fairy tales (*Rumpelstiltskin*), and myths (*The Magic Pitcher*) for a younger readership. Picture Parade was an educational publication aimed directly at schools; after the fourth issue, the name was changed to Picture Progress. The range of subjects covered history, science, geography, current events, and entertainment. After failing to attract enough interest from the school market at a time when the anti-comics campaign was at its peak, Picture Progress came abruptly to an end after twenty issues in the fall of 1955.

Unwilling to accept defeat, Albert Kanter turned his attention to a new educational venture, a series of ninety-six-page comic books, which would be issued twice a year and would be devoted to in-depth studies of specific subjects. The first Special Edition (later Special Issue) title, *The Story of Jesus*, No. 129A, would provide an emphatic demonstration of the difference between Classics Illustrated and other comics.

The idea of biblical comic books was not novel. In the 1940s, Max Gaines's seven-issue Picture Stories from the Bible had sold millions of copies. Two of the New Testament numbers from the series had been reprinted in 1945 as a ninety-six-page Complete Life of Christ. Atlas Comics had published five issues of Bible Tales for Young People from August 1953 to March 1954, while Famous Funnies had begun a four-issue run of Tales from the Great Book in February 1955.

Kanter was convinced that Classics Illustrated, with its reputation for quality and substance, could improve on the concept. He decided to commission a biography of Jesus based strictly on the four Gospels. It was important to him, as a man who cherished his Jewish faith and heritage, that the Classics Illustrated treatment be reverent toward the subject and respectful of the multiple Christian theological traditions.

Managing editor Meyer A. Kaplan hired Lorenz Graham, an African-American former missionary, to script the Special Edition. (Graham would later provide adaptations for Classics Illustrated No. 133, *The Time Machine*, and Classics Illustrated Special Issue No. 135A, *The Ten Commandments*.) The adaptation was faithful to the letter of the Authorized (King James) Version of the Bible. Daniel A. Poling, editor of the Christian Herald Magazine delivered a back-cover endorsement expressing his satisfaction "that the manuscript follows the gospel texts in the classic King James vernacular, and that it tells the immortal story, the greatest story ever told, without distortion or interpretation."

For the interior art, veteran Gilberton art director Alex A. Blum, who had illustrated such Classics Illustrated titles as *Alice in Wonderland* and *Treasure Island*, assisted William A. Walsh, the leading Classics Illustrated Junior artist whose credits included The Ugly Duckling and *Pinocchio*. The artists sought to render *The Story of Jesus* with a visual simplicity that would not detract from the message conveyed. Victor Prezio, who also supplied the painted cover for the Classics Illustrated edition of *Robin Hood*, produced a painted cover showing Jesus delivering the Sermon on the Mount. It was briefly replaced in a 1958 reprint with what collectors call the "Three Camels" cover, but Prezio's original subsequently returned in a 1961 edition.

With four printings, *The Story of Jesus* proved to be not only the most widely read of the Special Issues but also the most widely distributed of comic books with a religious theme. It was, indeed, as the Gilberton marketing phrase termed it, "The Classic of Classics."

CONTENTS

Adapted by
LORENZ GRAHAM

Illustrated by
WILLIAM A. WALSH
&
ALEX A. BLUM

CLASSICS *Illustrated* SPECIAL EDITION, *The Story of Jesus* Number 129A Adaptation by Lorenz Graham
"Jesus on the Mountain " Cover by Victor Prezio; interior art by William A. Walsh and Alex A. Blum
New digitalized artwork: Cover by Christina Choma and interior artwork by Susan Shaw-Russell, Leigh Young and Bruce Downey.
Published by JACK LAKE PRODUCTIONS INC. 5334 Yonge Street, Suite 902, Toronto, Ontario, Canada M2N 6V1
Copyright © 2004 First Classics, Inc. All Rights Reserved. Published with the written licensed permission of First Classics, Inc.
THIS BOOK FOR INTERNATIONAL DISTRIBUTION AND SALE.   www.jacklakeproductions.com   **Printed in Canada.**

THE STORY OF JESUS

Two thousand years ago, Rome had conquered almost all of the world that was known to her people. Roman emperor Caesar Augustus had set up puppet kings and appointed governors throughout the empire. He gave them armored legions to enforce Roman law and to collect taxes. The wealth of the conquered lands flowed to Rome.

On the far eastern shores of the Mediterranean, Caesar Augustus supported Herod the Great as king in Palestine, the home of the Jewish nation. Jerusalem, in the province of Judea, was Herod's capital. North of Judea lay the province of Galilee.

The Jews, who were sorely oppressed, hoped for a Messiah, a messenger from God, who would save their nation. Their prophets had promised such a leader.

It was in Bethlehem, a village of Judea, that Jesus was born.

Suddenly the Angel of the Lord came upon them and
His glory shone round them and they were afraid.

THE VISIT OF THE SHEPHERDS

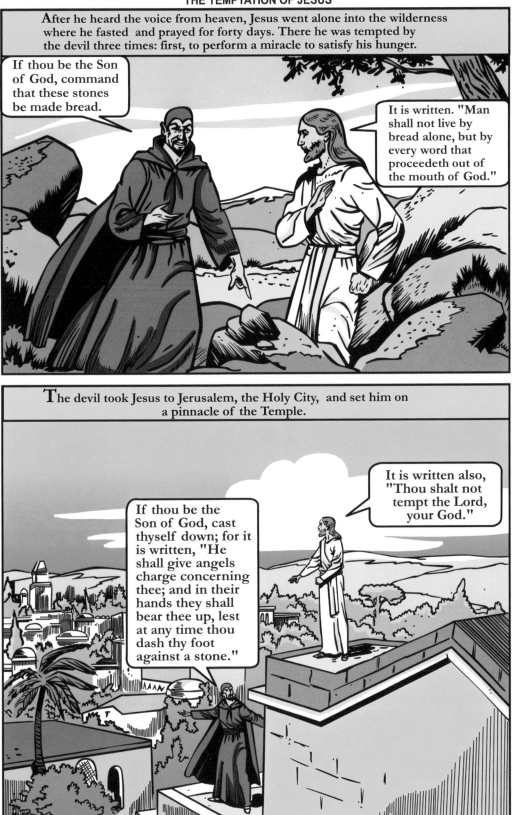

JESUS OVERCOMES TEMPTATION

THE CALLING OF DISCIPLES

Philip and Bartholomew, Thomas and Thaddeus, another James, not the son of Zebedee, and another Simon, not Peter, and Judas Iscariot, these were recruited at the beginning of Jesus' active work. They did not understand Jesus at first, but they believed in him and they loved him. Jesus ordained twelve, that they should be with him, and that he might send them forth to preach, and to have power to heal sicknesses and to cast out devils.

In Nazareth, his home, Jesus took his turn, as was the custom, to read from the Holy scriptures on the Sabbath day. He read the words of the prophet Isaiah.

"The spirit of the Lord is upon me, because he hath anointed me to preach the Gospel to the poor; He hath sent me to heal the brokenhearted, to preach deliverance to the captives, and recovering of sight to the blind, to set at liberty them that are bruised."

When he was through with his reading, he spoke to the congregation.

This day is this scripture fulfilled.

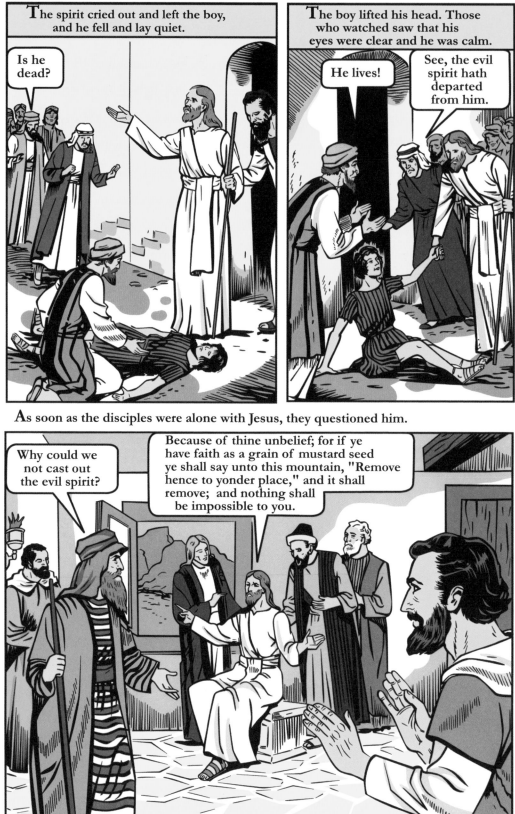

THE DOCTRINE OF LOVE

* Under the ancient Jewish Law, certain thank offerings were to be made for special healings.

THE PARABLE OF THE SOWER

Soon after they started, Jesus, being weary, slept.

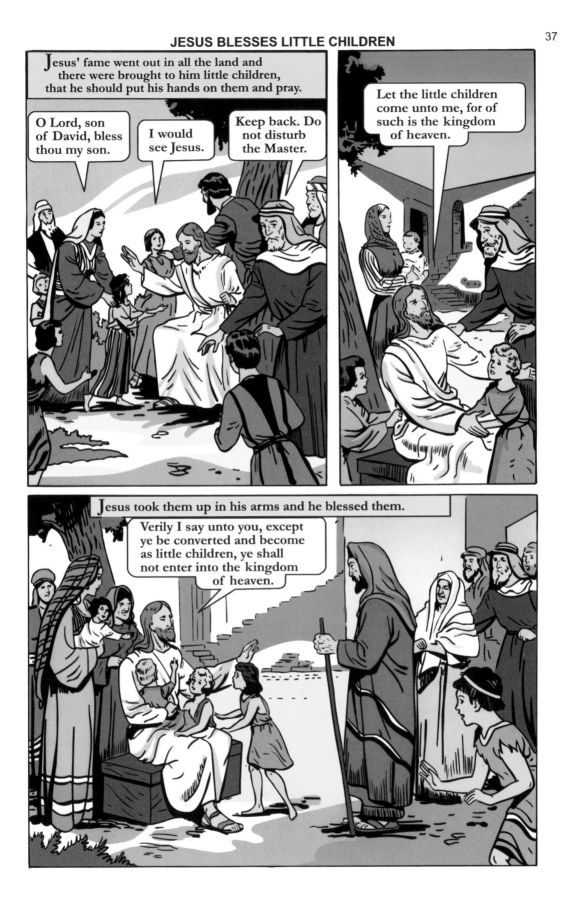

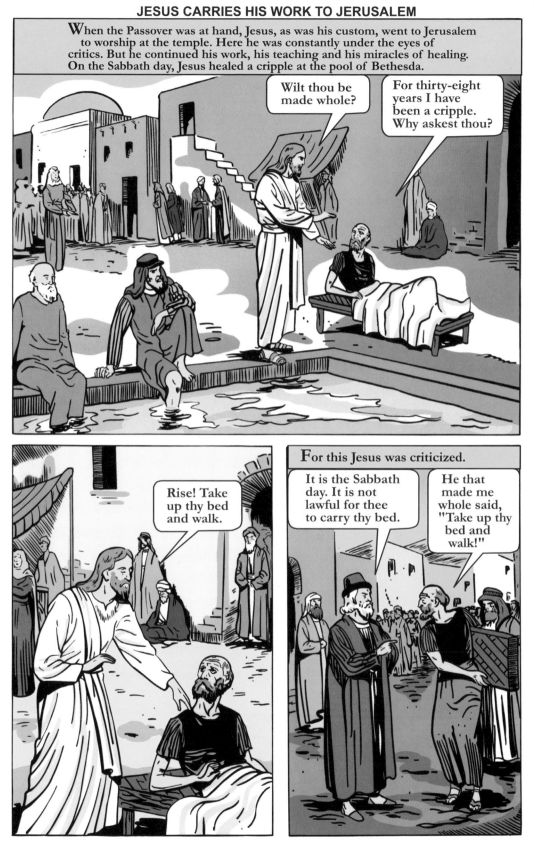

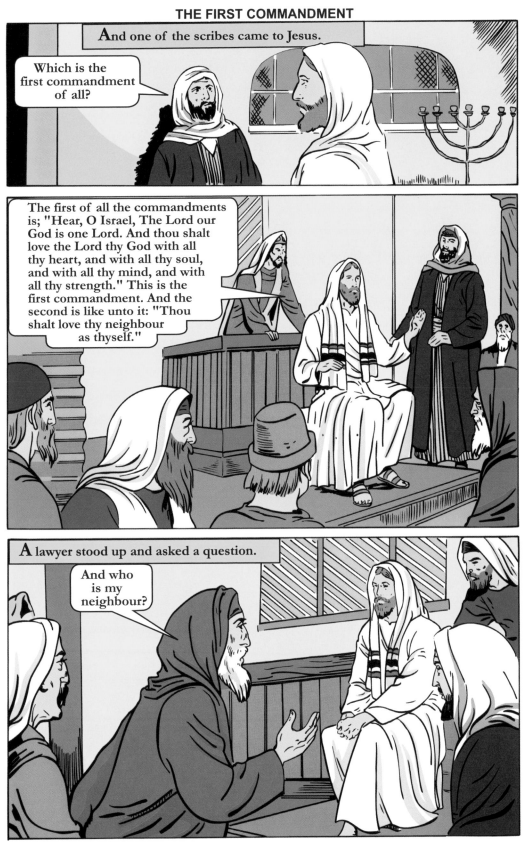

A certain man went down from Jerusalem to Jericho and fell among thieves who stripped him of his raiment* and wounded him and left him half dead.

*clothing

And by chance there came down a certain priest that way and when he saw him, he passed by on the other side.

And likewise a levite*, when he was at the place, came and looked and passed by on the other side.

* A scholar or temple attendant

"But a certain samaritan came, and when he saw him, he had compassion . . .

"And went to him and bound up his wounds, pouring in oil and wine.

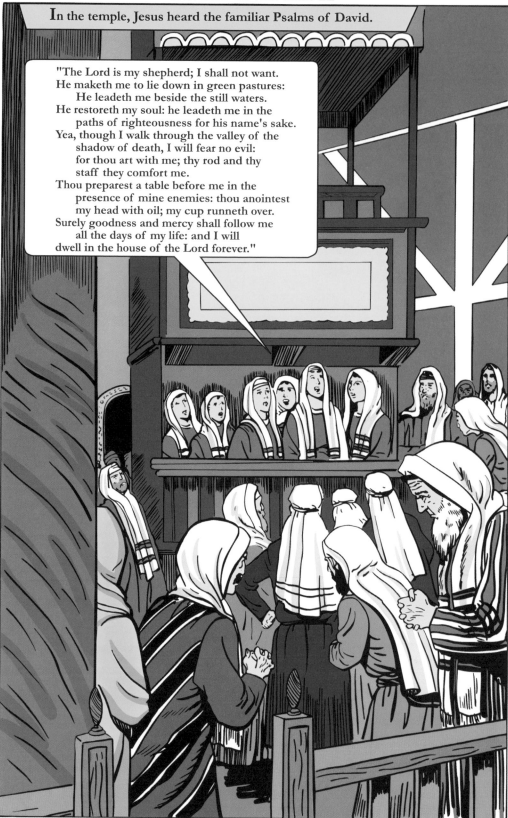

PETER'S CONFESSION

THE TRANSFIGURATION

Then Jesus charged his disciples that they should tell no man that he was the Christ, and he took Peter and James and John into a mountain.

While Jesus was praying before them his face shone as the sun and his garments became white as the light, and there appeared unto them Moses, the law giver, and Elijah, the prophet.

Lord, it is good to be here. Let us make three tabernacles. One for thee and one for Moses and one for Elijah.

A cloud overshadowed them and out of the cloud came a voice.

THIS IS MY BELOVED SON. HEAR HIM.

When the disciples heard the voice they were stricken with fear.

Arise and be not afraid.

The season of the holy days came again. Six days before the Passover, Jesus sat with Lazarus at supper. Martha served, but Mary anointed the feet of Jesus with ointment.

Why this waste? That precious ointment might have been sold for much money and given to the poor.

Let her alone. She is come to anoint my body to the burying.

THIRTY PIECES OF SILVER

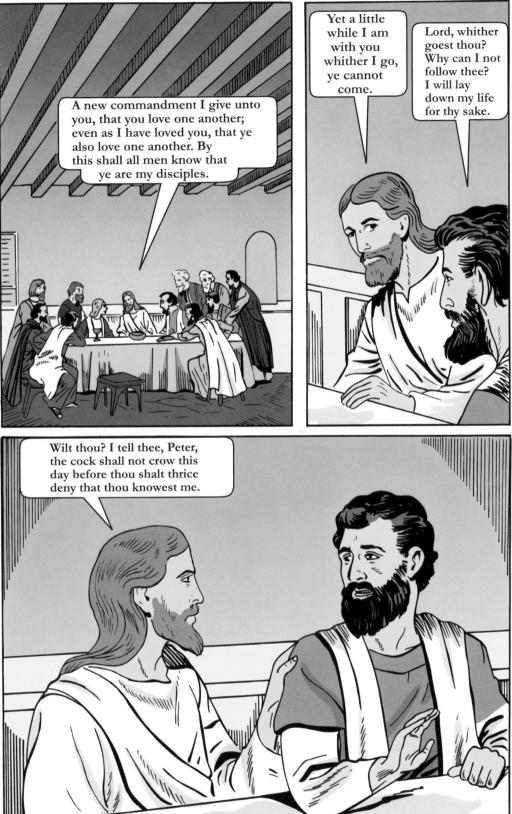

At a late hour, Jesus led his disciples out to the Mount of Olives across the brook Cedron, to a garden called Gethsemane. As they walked, he sought to comfort them.

Let not your heart be troubled. Ye believe in God, believe also in me. In my Father's house are many mansions. If it were not so, I would have told you. I go to prepare a place for you, I will come again and receive you unto myself, that where I am, there may ye be also.

Taking Peter, James and John with him, Jesus went a little further.

My soul is exceeding sorrowful. Tarry ye here and watch with me.

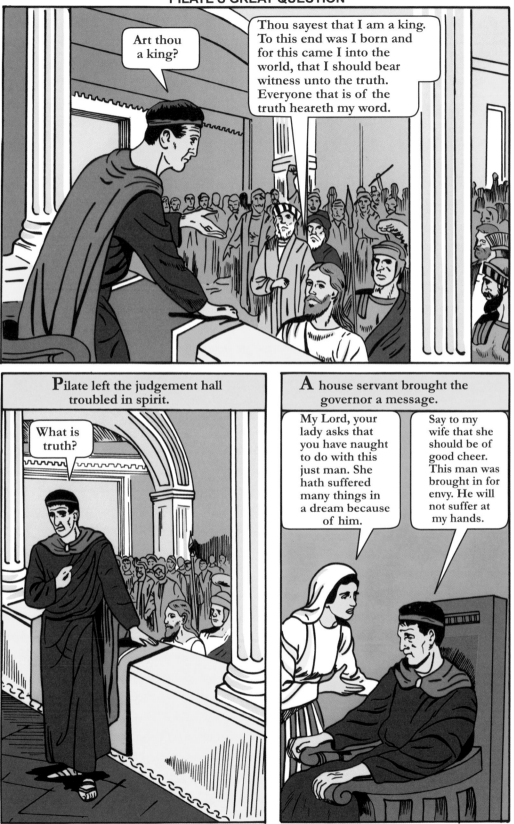

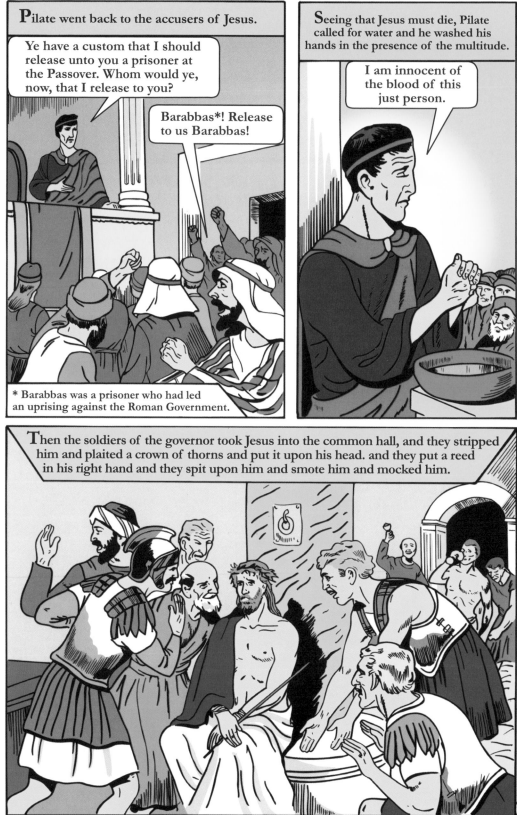

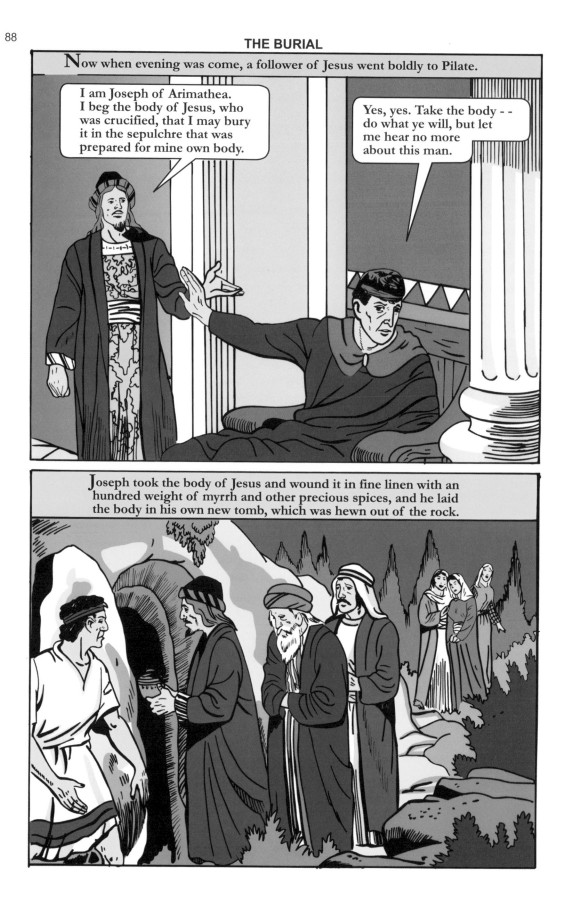

THE BURIAL

A great stone was rolled to the door of the sepulchre. The women which came from Galilee followed and they beheld the sepulchre and how Jesus' body was laid away.

THE EMPTY TOMB

THE DISCIPLES' DESPAIR

MARY MAGDALENE'S DISCOVERY

But when Mary Magdalene told the disciples, they would not believe.

I have seen him and he spoke to me and he said that I should tell thee that he must ascend unto his Father and our Father and to his God and our God.

She is but a woman and these are but idle tales that she believeth because of her grief.

Except I shall see in his hands the print of nails and thrust my hand into his side* - - I will not believe.

* To make sure Jesus was dead, one of the Roman soldiers had stabbed the body with a spear.

THE ASCENSION

Jesus led them out as far as Bethany. There, he lifted up his hands and blessed them, and it came to pass while he blessed them, he was parted from them and carried up into heaven.

There are many other things which Jesus did, which, if they should be written every one, the world itself could not contain the books that should be written.

AMEN